SHARE MY NAME!

Untold Stories of Persecution, Extortion, and Murder by the Muslim Brotherhood

BY
RIK DOIRSE
AND
SAMEH MASRY

Rev 12:11
Rik Doirse

ISBN: 978-1-939570-32-1
Copyright © 2013

Published by Word & Spirit Publishing
P.O. Box 701403
Tulsa, OK 74170

The authors may be contacted by mail at:
Share My Name
P.O. Box 123
Broken Arrow, OK 74013

A significant portion of the profits from book sales will be donated to assist in the planting and rebuilding of churches in Egypt and the Middle East.

CONTENTS

Preface v

Names and Terms..vii

PART 1: Stories of the Persecuted 1
    This Is Our Time! 2
    Everything Is So Obvious................................4
    Two Challenges 7
    The Case Is Documented.................................9
    A False Report..11
    It Just Looks Like Peace.................................13
    Deception and Cover-ups...............................16
    A Sworn Oath 18
    Acid Attack 23
    We Don't Like It at All 25
    Revenge on a Child 28
    Too Many Decrees...30
    This Tiny Place 32
    Spirit of the Revolution 34
    People Are Still Afraid.....................................36
    I Won't Follow Islam..38
    I Am on Your Side..40
    Such Love...43
    Musicians on the Titanic..................................45
    A Straightforward Question.............................48

It Is Her Fault...50
We Can't Do Anything....................................52
Supported by Police.......................................55
Anytime, Anywhere.......................................57
Hindering the Children 59
A Constant Threat..61
It Isn't Magical..63
The End of the World 66

PART 2: The Muslim Brotherhood and
the Revolution..69
Understanding What Has Happened
in Egypt...70
The Effect of Flawed Policies........................77
Postscript: The Syria Connection.................97

PREFACE

The stories within this book are the real-life experiences of those who live in Egypt's current turmoil. We had heard of people being kidnapped, extorted, beaten, robbed, raped, and locked inside of churches, but it seemed that no one was telling their stories. We knew it was important—even necessary—to collect their stories and share them with others who would care. Therefore, we set on a mission to meet as many of them as possible face-to-face and to look into their eyes as they told tell their stories.

As one of those interviewed so clearly stated, "The persecution began before the revolution." Before January 25, 2011, anyone could be a target of the regime's wrath. But after the revolution, the Christians in Egypt (about 18 percent of the population[1]) would come to find the persecution keenly focused upon them. The bureaucracy of a government without a code of laws provided a pathway for the majority to inflict insidious terror upon those in the minority.

The fear of reprisal is very real among Christians in Egypt. While several people consented to tell their stories, most who were invited chose not to do so. For those who were willing to meet with us, we explained that we did not want to know the names of churches, villages, or even their own identities. Our concern was that they might somehow become targeted and their persecutions and difficulties would increase. Still, some insisted on sharing that information. One pastor adamantly told us, "Share the name of my village, share the name of my church, and share my name! If someone finds out about us, what more can they do to us?" In the spirit of his request we have given a name to each of these brave believers, with the hope that we can put a "face" to each of these stories, while altering their real identities in order to protect their anonymity.

The stories that follow are taken from personal interviews with translation completed by native Arabic speakers. While the original intent was to provide a direct translation from Arabic to English, it became clear that many phrases and idioms needed further refinement to provide a clearer understanding and a more readable experience.

To the best of our ability, these stories are their stories. After you have read them, one of the best possible outcomes would be that their stories will become a part of your conversation with others and be integrated into times of personal and corporate prayer.

For those who gave permission for their stories to be told, their hope was not that others would feel sorry for them. Rather, they hope Christians around the world will continually send prayers before the throne of heaven and move the hand of God on their behalf.

—RIK DOIRSE AND SAMEH MASRY

NAMES AND TERMS

El-Ekwhan: The transliterated Arabic term for "the brotherhood," that is now used exclusively in reference to the Muslim Brotherhood. It is often interchanged with the terms "wicked," "wicked people," or "the wicked ones" and may also be used to describe gangs or thugs.

Put Their Hands on It: Refers to the action of squatters on a property. The property may be an open piece of land, a vacant building, or even a building that is in use. In some cultures, squatters' rights may be an adverse possession (a continuous, hostile, open, and actual possession to the exclusion of its true owner[2]) and can provide certain legal options.

Salafi: A movement among Sunni Muslims who follow a literal interpretation of ancient texts. The word comes from the Arabic word, Salafiyya, and originated from the term, al-salaf al-salih, which means, "the pious predecessors." It refers to the generations of Muslims who lived around the time of the Prophet Mohammed in the Seventh Century. It is considered the fastest growing Islamic movement in the world. Salafis are opposed to women or Christians serving in public office.

Lower/Middle/Upper Egypt: Because the Nile River flows from south to north, Egyptians have historically referred to the delta region in the north as Lower Egypt. Middle Egypt is the region between Memphis and Asyut. The remainder of the country, just south of Asyut, is considered Upper Egypt.

PART 1

STORIES OF THE PERSECUTED

"BLESSED ARE THOSE WHO ARE PERSECUTED
FOR RIGHTEOUSNESS' SAKE, FOR THEIRS IS
THE KINGDOM OF HEAVEN."
—MATTHEW 5:10

Ameer

THE HOLY SPIRIT IS PREPARING A REVIVAL IN
ALL OF EGYPT AND THE ENTIRE ARAB WORLD.

THIS IS OUR TIME!

Before the 25th of January Revolution, things were not easy. Now, most of those things that were not easy are not even possible. You must understand that the government allows those of the Muslim Brotherhood to do whatever they want. If they wanted, they could send 200 people here and close down this meeting. We could go to the police, but they would do nothing.

When my family goes to church, we take whatever kind of transportation we can find. We do not have a car. In our country, it is common to stand by the side of the road and wait for a driver to offer you a ride. But, Muslims can easily see that we are Christians, especially by the type of clothes our women wear. Most often they do not want to give us a ride.

I will be completely honest with you—not all Muslims are bad people. It is only those who are more radical, like those who are the Salafi or the Muslim Brotherhood that cause the problems. They go and talk to others (especially to the poorer people and those who are less educated) and tell them, "You cannot help a Christian. If you help a Christian, it is against our religion." Since those people don't fully understand, they will often tell us what others have said to them and then say to us, "This is what I have been told. No, I can't help you." This is true of our neighbors and even those who have been our friends.

But, this is our time! This is the time for the Christians in Egypt and the Arab world to decide what we will do. I believe the Holy Spirit is preparing a revival in all of Egypt and the entire Arab world. I believe this because I have been teaching leaders in Sudan, Jordan, and Egypt. I have been traveling to those places and teaching about evangelism, leadership, time management, and how to work with people. In many places, I see that this is our time. It may not be easy; but God will help us and He will help our churches.

Yasser

Whether in a neighborhood,
in a business, or even on the street,
if you are a Christian in Egypt,
you are an outcast.

EVERYTHING IS SO OBVIOUS

Egypt is a very different place since the revolution. It has become a very difficult country for Christians to live in. We are <u>treated as second-class citizens</u>. This is also true in my business. Because I am a Christian, my business is considered inferior by many Muslims.

Our church is in an area of Cairo with a high population density of Christians. At the moment, our Muslim neighbors are trying to start a fight with us while we are trying to show them our kindness and love. We are trying to be peaceful with them because we know that if we don't, they will become very harsh against us. However, they are trying to trap us.

We try to be polite, but to some Muslim men, we are not polite enough. They may try to start a fight for any reason. At the moment, it is not about the words you say or do not say. It is much more serious than that. These days it is about what tools can be used to limit you or stop you. Perhaps it is better to say it is about mind games and intimidation, tools, guns, and taking away property.

The neighborhood where our church is located is very poor and has become very rough. There is a fanatic Muslim leader living very close to the church. Not long ago, he started a big fight because the pastor did not use a Muslim greeting when he walked past him. Of course, it's normal that Christians prefer not to use Muslim greetings. But the problem is that if you don't say this greeting it will cause a problem with them. So, we have decided to ignore this fanatic Muslim. Instead of walking right in front of him, we now go a different way, a longer distance, in order to go around him.

While we may have some rights for ourselves or for our businesses, if those who are against us work for any official offices, they will try to stop us from even seeking justice. People look at us as if we are not welcome any more. Whether in a neighborhood, in a business, or even on the street, if you are a Christian in Egypt, you are an outcast. You are like a foreigner. Even though we originally were equal citizens of this great country, it's now like we have lost our citizenship completely. We have become strangers and are no longer welcome in our land.

We do have the right to vote, especially in Cairo and the larger cities. But, as you can imagine, the government of the El-Ekwhan, or the Muslim Brotherhood, likes to deal in their own ways with the ballot boxes. They have many ways of manipulating them. It is true that the former President Mubarak used to do the same things, but now they do it even more and it is very obvious. At least Mubarak was a diplomatic leader, but the El-Ekwhan doesn't have that kind of experience. Everything now is so obvious and forceful.

If I were to talk about the reality, the obvious reality, it's getting darker and darker. It's getting harder and harder. But we have faith. We keep praying and trusting that God will protect us, even though we have to be very cautious when we're moving from one place to another. But even with all of the difficulties, I still prefer to stay and live in Egypt.

By the way, we are very upset about the American government's policy of support for the El-Ekwhan and the fanatic Muslims. As Christians, we used to feel proud of America, but not anymore. At one time, America used to support the minority people. But what America is doing now with their support of the radicals and their lack of concern for the Christians is absolutely unfair.

Mourad

TWO CHALLENGES

I am from Cairo. We received a 220 square meter (2,368 square feet) donation of land by one of our Christian brothers from Giza. We thanked the Lord because it is an area without any evangelical churches. It made me happy to think that the first meeting in the church would be in association with the leading Pentecostal denomination in Egypt.

The first challenge for us was money because the work to build the church costs around 3 million Egyptian pounds ($140,000 USD). But when we started to collect some money to begin construction we faced the second challenge. From the very beginning, the fanatic Muslims have prevented us from putting in the foundation of the church. They tried to force us to sell it to them so they could put a mosque there instead. We have actually given up the land at that location and are choosing to locate the church in another place in order to avoid bloodshed.

Now we are praying to God and believing that He will see our situation more clearly and provide us with the resources necessary for us to build the church.

Amal

> WHY DID THEY PUT THAT POISON IN THE
> FISH? BECAUSE THEY DON'T LIKE CHRISTIANS.

THE CASE IS DOCUMENTED

The persecution began before the revolution.

One year when we celebrated Easter, we were eating some salted fish. Because the Muslims were fasting on those days, they could not eat this kind of fish. They would eat it on the regular days but not on the fasting days because it makes them thirsty. But, they knew the Christians would eat it, so the Muslim Brotherhood put some poison—botulism—in the fish so that when the Christians would eat it, they would get sick.

I am one of those who were poisoned. I have copies of the newspapers and a magazine from those times when I was poisoned. I was so sick that I had to be admitted to the hospital. The government arranged for medicine to be brought from Germany because we did not have that kind of medicine here in Egypt.

9

My mother and sister died. My sister was pregnant. Both of them died of the same poison and I nearly died. Many families in an area of Cairo with a high-density population of Christians had people who died at that time. It was a terrible time. Some people got better, but many people died because they did not have the money for the medicine. But what did the officials do about this incident? They closed the investigation! Nothing was ever done about it. Everything was finished and they closed the case without any charges made against anyone.

Again, this was documented in magazines and the newspapers throughout Egypt. The story is well-documented. Why did they put that poison in the fish? Because they don't like Christians.

Tarek

> WHO SHALL SEPARATE US FROM THE LOVE OF
> CHRIST? SHALL TRIBULATION, OR DISTRESS,
> OR PERSECUTION, OR FAMINE, OR NAKEDNESS,
> OR PERIL, OR SWORD? AS IT IS WRITTEN:
> "FOR YOUR SAKE WE ARE KILLED ALL DAY
> LONG; WE ARE ACCOUNTED AS SHEEP FOR THE
> SLAUGHTER." YET IN ALL THESE THINGS WE
> ARE MORE THAN CONQUERORS THROUGH
> HIM WHO LOVED US. (ROMANS 8:35-37)

A FALSE REPORT

May I tell you a very real story about our church? Because it is in a central, major business area, the pastor thought it would be a good idea to have a medical clinic in the church. He brought in about ten beds for sick people or anyone who had been hurt or shot in the protests. People could very quickly take them to that clinic in the church.

11

However, a Muslim television broadcast started falsely reporting that the clinic didn't provide medical care for the people. Instead, they said the church was giving them heroin. Within a very short time after that false report was aired, some people started throwing Molotov cocktails at the church.

Just last week, the radicals burned a Christian school very close to the church. Actually, one school was bombed and burned with Molotov cocktails and a second school was also bombed and burned two weeks earlier. But, the church has not been hurt in any way.

Our pastor is a very well-known person here in Egypt. Actually, he is known all over the Arab world. He is the pastor of an evangelical church and their meetings are broadcast directly by satellite all over the world.

Ashraf

IT JUST LOOKS LIKE PEACE

I am 80 years old and an elder at a church in an area of
Cairo with a high percentage of Christians living there.
Our church has been badly affected by the revolution.
Many churches were affected badly because of the revo-
lution—if you'd like to call it a "revolution."

One church, which I know very well, had an empty space
of land. They were planning to expand their church and
to build on the land or to just extend their present church
building onto the land they owned. But because the
church has some fanatic Muslim neighbors, and they
don't like at all to hear the Christian prayers, they came
and attacked it. They "put their hands on it" or claimed
it as squatters. What I mean to say is that they took over
the property and said, "We must build a mosque here."

13

Not only are they stopping us, but they are even violating our possessions right in front of us. And they are insulting us, which only adds to the injury they are inflicting upon us.

The Muslim radicals are the government. They are the police. They have all the documents. Whatever documents they need are ready for them. Today it is actually very serious. If you are a radical Muslim and you come to this land and say, "This is mine. I'm ready to kill anyone for it!" then that's it. It is finished. The land will be yours.

Our government will have nothing to do with handling things like that. Actually, this is what they do. They will bring a pastor or Coptic priest and a Muslim leader together and ask them to sit together, shake hands, and act as if they are all at peace together. But, it just looks like peace—it is sort of like peace, but it is only for the news media and only for the moment. As soon as the moment is over, the radical Muslims are right back attacking the Christians again as if nothing had ever happened. That is because nothing really did happen. It was just a show.

But there is something happening right now in Egypt, which to me is the most important thing. When the persecution came against Christians in Egypt, it made many come back again to the Lord and be united as one—all denominations are coming together. Actually, this is what's happening at the moment. The Coptic, Catholic, and Protestant churches have come together as one and are united in Christ.

Youssef

DECEPTION AND COVER-UPS

At the hospital where I work, I have seen the personnel change the police reports so that nobody can blame the Muslim Brotherhood for any injuries. I have actually witnessed a change of the cause of death for a person that was clearly murdered. The death certificate said that someone died of a heart problem, when it was obvious he was beaten by wooden sticks, or boards, or poles, or something else. I know of one man who was brought to the hospital that had been shot multiple times. His cause of death was listed as suicide. It's very easy for them to change the cause of death.

And, if someone were to challenge the report or file a complaint to the police station, they are ignored. The police won't write a complaint or even open an investigation. It is because an investigation would expose the

Muslim Brotherhood for who they really are. They are wicked and only care for themselves and for those who are like them.

Hatem

> YES, AND ALL WHO DESIRE TO LIVE GODLY IN
> CHRIST JESUS WILL SUFFER PERSECUTION.
> (2 TIMOTHY 3:12)

A SWORN OATH

Our church is in Middle Egypt. I am the pastor and have served this church for six years. The church building is small, about 50 square meters (550 square feet). The neighbors are Muslims from the Salafi, which are the fanatic Muslims. They are the Muslims who believe they should be the rulers of Egypt.

The Salafi have been attacking us in many different ways for some time. For example, before the revolution they would regularly put a loudspeaker with a microphone up against the church. They would be making loud announcements or would say their prayers over the loud-speaker just to make it difficult for us while we were holding our meetings.

18

After the revolution, they started dealing with us in a very harsh way. They have brought in many, many fanatic Muslim people. Some of them are even more radical and carry weapons like knives and machetes with them wherever they go.

One day while we were holding our service, a group of radicals brought a chain and locked us in the church while we were in it. Our people became very frightened. We are people of faith, but we live in a world where everyone does not believe the same as we do. We were afraid that the radical Muslims would begin throwing Molotov cocktails or some type of bomb in through the windows. With the doors locked from the outside, no one from the inside would be able to escape.

Some people from the church tried to open the doors, but the chief of the radical group wouldn't allow us to get out of the church. It took about two hours of begging him to let us get out of the church and go back home to our homes before he finally allowed us to do so.

In the end, they came to the point where they made this demand: "You must remove the loudspeakers from inside your church and give them to us." The reason was that they did not want the sound of our voices to get outside of the church by any means.

The radical Muslims have said, "We have made a promise to remove all churches from our land. Egypt is a

Muslim land." More than a promise, they have made a vow and sworn an oath that there will not be any Christian presence in Egypt.

These people have even gone to the police and reported that I was a terrorist. So I went and told the police officer all that was happening to us. I told him that we as a people, and as a nation, should be better after the revolution, not worse. He answered, "Thank you, dear pastor, for the polite way that you speak with me." He advised me to not make any conflict with the Salafi because he couldn't defend us or even defend himself. His words were a very big surprise to me.

After that, we couldn't even make an official complaint against the radicals because we didn't want to make any more problems with them. But they continue to find ways to abuse us and continue trying to force us from our church. Apart from putting our problem before God, we have no solution and no protection because we don't have a working government at the moment.

Right now, there are about 50 people who are a part of our church. We meet in small cell groups in our village. We sometimes have prayer meetings at the church and a few people come to it. We still use the old building, but not for any general meetings. We have been divided into cell groups just in case others get to know where we are meeting and cause problems.

We don't have any members among us in our church that are rich or any wealthy businessmen who can help to support us. We are all poor people who live in a farming community. We all have very small incomes. We have received some money from people who love God in order to buy another piece of land somewhere else. We are now constructing this new building in a way that is you might call "underground"—or secretly. That way, none of these people can see in case they should learn what we are doing and push us away from the new land.

We don't have any permission to build, so we have to do it secretly. The truth is, there is no official permission available anymore. There is no place to go to get permission. We don't have a government right now. We will try to collect official documents to prove that this land is set aside as a place to worship God, but we will see what happens.

We shared this matter with a friend from the U.S. and he kindly supported us with some financial help. But now we don't have any money at all to finish the first floor with cement. It is not wise to sell our current building right now. Others will immediately realize that we are building something else. If we tried to sell it will not bring much money. It is one more way they would keep us from having a new building.

What does the future hold for the Church in Egypt? I believe God has promised He will show His glory through the church. What I mean by this is that He will be changing people and filling them with his Spirit. In my mind, this is the real glory of God; changed lives filled with the power of the Holy Spirit.

Hana

ACID ATTACK

My very dear friend is a lay leader and Sunday School teacher at her church. Recently, she was walking in her neighborhood. There was a man following her and he kept calling out terrible insults to my friend. She tried to pay no attention to him but he kept following and saying horrible things to her.

While trying to mind her own business, he came up from behind and threw a container filled with acid on her back. The acid melted her clothes, burned her hair, and left horrible burns on the back of her head, neck, and back. Now she is in extreme pain from the burns and is afraid to leave her apartment. She needs to go to the hospital for treatment, but she is afraid to even go outside for fear that the man will see her again and may try to kill her or her family.

The reason why my friend was targeted is because of her evangelical beliefs. The man who threw the acid on her is a fanatic Muslim.

Karim

THERE IS SUCH HUNGER TO HEAR THE
GOOD NEWS.

WE DON'T LIKE IT AT ALL

Unless something miraculous happens, I think our country will be destroyed by the ignorant Muslim Brotherhood. They think that we now have "law" because they have come to power. They have illegally lowered the age of marriage for girls to just nine years old. For "education," they want to devote females to just practice sex. They want to go back hundreds of years to the Dark Ages—to the time of Mohammed. We are astonished at this.

But the good news is that Muslims have started to think and ask questions. They are asking things like, "Is this really Islam? What kind of a religion is this that we are dealing with? Is this the way I want to live the rest of my life? Do I want to teach this to my children?" Many of them have begun to change their minds about Islam.

Some did not think of God outside of Islam at all before the revolution, but now some have become Christians. A lot of people are also seeking Christianity on the Internet. At our church, Muslim ladies come to the service and remove their veils. Afterwards, before they go back home from the service, they go into the bathrooms and put the veils back on.

There are rules for selling books and Holy Bibles. Actually, a lot of Muslims were buying them during the revolution. Now, an increasing number of Muslims are buying Bibles and seeking the true God. This is good news. They don't experience the persecution like we do but they see the truth and the blessings we have and they wonder how it is possible. They have been told that Christianity is a false religion. But when they see God blessing us, they begin to wonder if what they have been told is not true.

It's easier for us during conversation now to talk about Christianity. Of course, we are still afraid to share the Good News with a Muslim. Only if a Muslim asks us can we answer, but we cannot initiate a conversation or volunteer to tell them. When we are reading the newspaper, we can tell them, "Even this is what is written by the prophet," or "This is what is written in the Bible about the end of days." That's how we're starting to share with our colleagues and others.

There is such hunger to hear the Good News. People in Egypt were anxiously waiting until Islamic law was established because they thought we were living under a government with so much corruption. They thought it was like that because Islamic law was not established. But when they saw what a true Islamic government looks like, now they are saying, "No, we don't like Islam at all." You can read those very words in the newspaper. That is what they say. As Christians, we are astonished to see Muslim people in the television broadcasts refusing and rejecting Islam.

We know that Egypt was leading the Arab countries before the revolution in everything. In teaching and medical progress—everything was started by Egypt. We are a very critical country and that's why we know something will change. We don't know exactly what, but we think something will happen and suddenly things will change. And, when that happens, we believe a lot of people will come to know Jesus in all the Arab countries.

Mariam

REVENGE ON A CHILD

My beautiful niece, Jessie, was only 10 years old when she was shot in the heart and killed by one of the "El-Ekwhan." The Muslim Brotherhood has promised to get their revenge on the Christians. They said our families, our children, our homes and businesses would be destroyed. They believe only Christians are responsible for President Morsi being taken from his office.

Jessie had been attending a Vacation Bible School and was walking home with her teacher. Because of the many difficulties we now have in Egypt, Jessie was holding her teacher's hand as they walked. It was after 7:00 in the evening on August 6, 2013. It was the end of the ninth day of a 10-day program.

So, on that evening, they took their revenge on a young girl. Suddenly, out of nowhere, a shot rang-out. One moment, she was alive and talking with her teacher. In the next moment, she was dead from a gunshot to the heart—killed by a supporter of the former president, Mr. Morsi.

Jessie was the only child of my sister and her husband. They were devastated.

Now, they are praying for those who killed their daughter. God has given them a love for those who killed her, and they pray for the terrorists, the land of Egypt, and for all of our people more than ever before.

Ala

TOO MANY DECREES

We had the proper documents, including the presidential decree, and were doing some remodeling work on our church in Upper Egypt. We were almost finished—except for the wall that goes around the church on the outside. In order to finish it, we were told we needed to have another Presidential Decree.

We received the second decree but after a while, someone started to make a case about it. They said it wasn't right to have two presidential decrees for one place. They said that if I didn't pay 1,000 Egyptian Pounds ($140 USD), I would go to prison for three months.

One of my friends said, "No, don't pay anything." In the end, we were surprised that the judge dismissed the case and I didn't have to pay anything. It appeared that it was the Lord's hand at work.

At the police station, they asked me, "Are you the pastor of the church?" I said, "No, I am just one from the people responsible in the church." Then they said, "Since you are not the pastor of the church, but just an employee, just forget about the wall issue."

It was only the Lord's hand that helped me. It is a hard time in Egypt and it seems like everyone is against the Christians. Everyone in my home was praying for me and God was glorified through the situation.

Emad

> "WHY HAVE YOU BROUGHT ME HERE TO THIS SPECIFIC PLACE? HAVE YOU BROUGHT ME TO DIE HERE?"

THIS TINY PLACE

I am a pastor. I established a church in Alexandria, very close to a Salafi mosque. It is one of the biggest Salafi mosques in Alexandria. When I got that tiny place to start a ministry, it was by God's hand. I spent a lot of time before God in order to make my decision about starting this church. For me, the decision was like life or death and the Lord gave me a very specific word about what I was to do.

In 2 Chronicles chapter 22, we read the story about David preparing to build the temple. Just like He spoke to David, God spoke to me very clearly about where I should start the church. It really was a very specific word from God and what He spoke to me stopped all my fear.

I used to ask God, "Why have you brought me here to this specific place? Have you brought me to die here?" One day I sensed the Lord telling me, "Satan has been worshiped in this land for years and years. I have given you this tiny place to glorify and to declare my name here in this land. Those people who cause such fear in your heart will one day be your disciples."

With God's help, we have finished building the place where we meet. It was opened just recently and we worshiped God there. I trust God's word to me that one day He will bring them to become His disciples in that place. Please pray that God will protect our tiny place. We don't know what the Salafi might do in the future, but we believe that God is going to protect us.

Isaac

> FOR IT IS GOD WHO WORKS IN YOU TO WILL
> AND TO ACT IN ORDER TO FULFILL HIS GOOD
> PURPOSE. (PHILIPPIANS 2:13 NIV)

SPIRIT OF THE REVOLUTION

It is very clear to everyone in Egypt that the revolution which happened in the Arab world has had a negative effect in the churches. From my point of view, the spirit of the revolution entered the churches and opened the way for the thugs to put pressure on believers. They steal money from Christians and deal with believers in a very harsh way. Consequently, so many, especially the sisters, are frightened by them and in that way they are being prevented from going to the church.

We are living in a dark season now under the Muslim Brotherhood rule. But God may bring blessing through it all. This will happen if we will come together in unity and live a life dedicated to God that pleases him. God will do a lot of things if we remind ourselves of the

Apostle Paul's words in Philippians 2:13, "For it is God who works in you to will and to act in order to fulfill his good purpose."

Daoud

> Do not fear any of those things which you are about to suffer. Indeed, the devil is about to throw some of you into prison, that you may be tested, and you will have tribulation ten days. Be faithful until death, and I will give you the crown of life. (Revelation 2:10)

PEOPLE ARE STILL AFRAID

I am an elder in a church in an area of Cairo with a high-density population of Christians. Our church used to have about 12 adult women and 12 adult men. We also had a very good children's ministry, Sunday school, and a youth ministry.

In the beginning of the revolution, the people who had been prisoners were released from prison and became very wicked people. They used to come and attack our business places and steal expensive things like mobile phones, clothing, and other items from all of the stores. In the days that followed, the mosques announced that if anyone had stolen anything, please bring those items to the mosque, because the owners needed to have them back.

Some of these wicked people hid many of things they had stolen and brought back some of the other things to the mosques. They believed the leaders of the mosque would take the items back to the owners. But when they came to know that all of those things would not be given back to the owners, they came and attacked some of the mosques to take back what they had already surrendered.

We had such fear in the beginning. Now, many people are still afraid and many people have stopped coming to the church. Women feel very insecure and have stopped coming from their apartments to go shopping or even come to the church. Because we have no security at the moment, or even police, these wicked people have come to have control over others. They came to a Christian man I know, made false accusations against him, and forced him to not open his shop anymore.

Before the revolution, more people attended our church than attend today. Some people used to come from a long distance and now they are afraid to come anymore at all. Now, we have about four or five men and four or five women who attend the services at our church.

Shaker

But I want you to know, brethren, that the things which happened to me have actually turned out for the furtherance of the gospel, so that it has become evident to the whole palace guard, and to all the rest, that my chains are in Christ; and most of the brethren in the Lord, having become confident by my chains, are much more bold to speak the word without fear. (Philippians 1:12-14)

I WON'T FOLLOW ISLAM

There is such fear in Christians' hearts toward the Muslims. Right now there is also such eagerness and earnestness in Muslims' hearts to come to know Jesus Christ. But we as Christians have such fear about telling them.

Even on television and radio talk shows, Muslims come against one another saying, "If our Islam is like that I won't follow it anymore." But, this is the Islam that they follow. We have never seen this type of disagreement before now. Even though they may disagree with each other, they still turn all of their anger and disappointments against the Christians.

Melad

> REPAY NO ONE EVIL FOR EVIL. HAVE REGARD FOR GOOD THINGS IN THE SIGHT OF ALL MEN. IF IT IS POSSIBLE, AS MUCH AS DEPENDS ON YOU, LIVE PEACEABLY WITH ALL MEN. BELOVED, DO NOT AVENGE YOURSELVES, BUT RATHER GIVE PLACE TO WRATH; FOR IT IS WRITTEN, "VENGEANCE IS MINE, I WILL REPAY," SAYS THE LORD. THEREFORE "IF YOUR ENEMY IS HUNGRY, FEED HIM; IF HE IS THIRSTY, GIVE HIM A DRINK; FOR IN SO DOING YOU WILL HEAP COALS OF FIRE ON HIS HEAD." DO NOT BE OVERCOME BY EVIL, BUT OVERCOME EVIL WITH GOOD. (ROMANS 12:17-21)

I AM ON YOUR SIDE

One day as I was out doing errands, I received a phone call from brothers in the church. They told me, "Please don't be upset when you return to your home. A person who lives next to the church has broken the door to your home."

When I got home, I was calm and began to ask what happened. I was told that a young man had done it. His father told me his son was a psychiatric patient and he had broken the door and the light in front of the church. At this time, I was perhaps too calm and told the father that, as the pastor of the church, I needed to speak with the police about the situation. At that point, the father started to speak very impolitely and even began swearing at me. The boy's mother and some of the other family members became a part of conversation and wouldn't let me go. The brothers from the church advised me not to spend the night in my home but I insisted on staying there.

From the beginning I was thinking about the issue with a troubled heart and felt a godly sorrow for them. Then I spoke with a friend who told me not to fight with the people because Satan could use them to embarrass me. Afterwards, I started to pray with authority. By faith, I knew they were nothing compared to the Lord who was with me. I prayed that the Lord would restrict Satan from further attacks.

Two days later, I passed in front of their home and we didn't speak to each other. But on the third day, I felt that I had to care for them as a pastor—even if they were unbelievers and harassing us. The family lived next door to the church and they could make things difficult with me personally or with our church members.

I went to the father and firmly started to explain to him that I should inform the police of what happened. But, because of Jesus' love and since his son was sick, I preferred not go to them. I also told him that he should not have spoken to me as he did. The father apologized and was so kind to me. I saw that the son seemed very nervous and upset so I took him in my arms and told him, "I love you and I am on your side." I told him this in front of his father and the son started to relax and be quiet.

Later, when we started to tear down the church to rebuild it, one of the other sons of this father wanted to complain about us to the police. But the father went to the son and prevented him from issuing a complaint against us. Now, they treat us politely. We have faced normal challenges during the rebuilding of the church but God gives us grace and everything is okay.

Thanks be to God.

Nagla

AFTER READING SOME OF THE SCRIPTURES,
SHE SAID, "THERE IS SUCH LOVE IN
THE BIBLE!"

SUCH LOVE

Just one week ago, I attended a conference here in Egypt. A young woman sat next to me and told me, "I was a Muslim. I have been married to four Muslim men and each one of them used to beat me very badly and treated me in a very harsh way."

This woman has been divorced four times. She was invited by a Christian businessman to attend his daughter's wedding. It was a long distance from her home, so they offered her a place to sleep at their home. When she went to bed, she lifted her pillow and saw a Bible and started reading it. After reading some of the scriptures, she said, "There is such love in the Bible!" She asked if she could have the Bible to read and she received Jesus Christ as her own savior.

The Lord is helping her as she follows after Him. She lives with her daughter in a home that she rents. She has become a tailor and earns enough money to cover all of her expenses.

It is not an easy thing for a woman to have a job. It is especially difficult for a woman to make enough money to cover all of her expenses. She gives glory to God for His help and is growing in Him day by day.

Youhana

THERE ARE SOME CHRISTIANS WHO FEEL
THEY ARE TO BE LIKE THE MUSICIANS ON
THE TITANIC. THEY WILL STAY UNTIL THE
VERY LAST.

MUSICIANS ON THE TITANIC

Life in Egypt is worse now than it was before the revolution. There are no laws. We are living in a bizarre manner. Anyone can stop you in the street and take your money, take your gold, or take your bag. There is so much corruption.

In a church near Tahrir Square, they treated people in a clinic at the church. But unfortunately, there is a lot of terrorism at the church. A lot of people don't attend the church today because they're afraid. They see the problems on the television and prefer to not attend at this time.

These days are very difficult for Christians. We are suffering. We are afraid even for the money in the bank. No one can guarantee that they won't take it because you

45

are an enemy in the eyes of fanatic Muslims. We are concerned that one day a man will come into power and say, "Christians are forbidden to transfer their money or take their money from the bank." We don't know, but we are afraid it is possible.

A lot of Christians are emigrating to other countries. They are leaving because they are afraid for what might happen to their children or even to themselves. But there are some Christians who feel they are to be like the musicians on the Titanic. They will stay until the very last. Do you know about those musicians? They were still playing, even as the ship sank. Christians are still here and they will continue playing, even during this corruption. But we are not safe.

Perhaps, because of some bad or unwise teaching, we thought we were protected. But this, of course, is not true for the situation. Christians are now kidnapped, raped, and even killed.

We have changed our minds and we now think this is the persecution the Bible speaks about that will come about in the Last Days. We realize that we may be persecuted or even killed, but we will continue to have faith in God.

Morcous

"But when you hear of wars and rumors of wars, do not be troubled; for such things must happen, but the end is not yet. For nation will rise against nation, and kingdom against kingdom. And there will be earthquakes in various places, and there will be famines and troubles. These are the beginnings of sorrows. But watch out for yourselves, for they will deliver you up to councils, and you will be beaten in the synagogues. You will be brought before rulers and kings for My sake, for a testimony to them. And the gospel must first be preached to all the nations." (Mark 13:7-10)

A STRAIGHTFORWARD QUESTION

There was an event that was very upsetting that happened recently in Alexandria. A man used to send some money back to Egypt to buy land while he was working abroad. His brothers bought the land for him and they decided to set part of it aside for the Lord in order to build a church.

Some fanatic Muslim people heard about it and went to visit the man's brothers. They acted as if they wanted to introduce themselves as neighbors. But they put a drug into the cups of the tea they were drinking that caused the brothers to fall asleep. When they were all asleep, the Muslim men shot them. That man lost all of his brothers.

The revolution has been a bad thing. Now, there is also a terrible problem with the kidnapping of many of our girls. Most of the Christians here would like to leave Egypt and would like to emigrate to America. Many of us have withdrawn all of our money from the bank for one purpose—to leave the country.

Yesterday, we heard that a Coptic church had an event and many people were traveling together on a bus. The bus was attacked by wicked people and they were forced to surrender and give up all that they had, including all their money.

We thank God that you have come safely to Egypt. We ourselves had such fear just to come from our cities to Alexandria. However, how much more difficult it must have been for you to come from America!

May I ask you a question? It is a very straightforward question. We know it's very obvious that the government in America supports the Muslim Brotherhood in Egypt. We do not understand it. Does your government really understand what they are doing? Why does America support the very ones who persecute the Christians?

Abd-El-Massih

A WOMAN COULD PROVE HER INNOCENCE BY
HAVING TWO WITNESSES TESTIFY ON HER
BEHALF. . . . NOW, ANYONE CAN DO
ANYTHING WITH ANY WOMAN, ANYWHERE.

IT IS HER FAULT

A good friend of mine is a pastor of a church in another village. He told me some men attacked a lovely young girl while she was walking in that village. They tried to strip off her clothes and forcibly have sex with her. They tried to rape her in public. They were not successful in doing so, but had they been successful, they would have accused her of having sex outside of marriage.

This is true. You may not believe it, but it is true. They would say it is her fault. That is exactly what they would do.

We used to have a law in Egypt that said a woman could prove her innocence by having two witnesses testify on her behalf. We do not have that law anymore. Now, anyone can do anything with any woman, anywhere. The wicked people who do these things will then threaten the woman's family. They will tell them to say that nothing happened to their daughter or to the lady in their house or else they will cause them even more serious problems.

At the moment, another thing that is very common is the kidnapping of young men and older men for one purpose; to abuse them and demand money. The kidnappers physically abuse them—beating, stabbing, cutting, and torturing them. And if they or their families don't pay any money, then they kill them. What I'm telling you now is very common in Egypt.

Bolous

> BELOVED, DO NOT BE SURPRISED AT THE
> FIERY TRIAL WHEN IT COMES UPON YOU TO
> TEST YOU, AS THOUGH SOMETHING STRANGE
> WERE HAPPENING TO YOU. BUT REJOICE
> INSOFAR AS YOU SHARE CHRIST'S SUFFERINGS,
> THAT YOU MAY ALSO REJOICE AND BE GLAD
> WHEN HIS GLORY IS REVEALED. IF YOU
> ARE INSULTED FOR THE NAME OF CHRIST,
> YOU ARE BLESSED, BECAUSE THE SPIRIT OF
> GLORY AND OF GOD RESTS UPON YOU.
> (1 PETER 4:12-14 ESV)

WE CAN'T DO ANYTHING

When I first went to serve the church in a small village near Minya in Middle Egypt, the church facility was not in very good condition. It was only 45 square meters (484 square feet) and was inside of a home.

Eventually, the owner of the home donated it so we started to find a way that we could make a separate door between it and the home. We started to receive offerings and bought a 50 square meter area (540 square feet) beside the church. We wanted to buy it because our village is full of Muslims and our congregation had about 70 people, including children. We are the only church in the village.

The exterior walls were made with some very old wood that had been roughly cut. We received permission to build three floors on the property and I started to work with the mayor of the village. He told me, "You will not be able to do anything in the church." I told him that I received the proper papers and everything was okay. But that was not the problem.

After the revolution, there was a strong challenge against us by the radical Muslims, the Salafis, in constructing the new building. I knew what had happened in a neighboring village. There was a place where Christians wanted to make a social center to serve both the Christians and the Muslims. When the Salafis found out about it, they took over the building and made it a mosque.

In another village, a church had received the permissions they needed to just do some remodeling. When the Salafis found out, they called one another and started to demonstrate around the church. When the governor went to the church and found the Salafis demonstrating, he cancelled his permission for the remodeling.

So the mayor told me, "Go to the police and ask them to protect you against the Salafis." When I went to the police, they said, "The mayor knows we can't do that." We went several times to ask for their help. Each time, they gave us some excuse or some reason why they had to delay their help.

We went back to the mayor and told him what had happened. He said, "Believe me, what you are doing is okay with me but I can't protect you against the fanatics. I know there are people who attend the church and who pray there. But we don't know what might happen. You may finish the building but someone may come and close the church totally and no one will be able enter it again."

This is our situation. We have all of the papers and permission we need. We have spent thousands of Egyptian pounds to get the right documents. And though everything was legally done, we can't do anything.

This is Egypt today.

Adel

SUPPORTED BY POLICE

Recently, members from our Presbyterian church were working and building the first and second floor of our building. The Salafis came against us and wanted to demolish one of the two floors that had just been completed. Actually, they wanted to demolish the entire church and rebuild it as a mosque. Now the building process is stopped. Even the bricks and blocks for building have not been able to be taken inside. They beat many Christians and physically injured some of them. In all of this, the police supported them.

Please believe me. I do not lie to you.

Some strong and powerful Muslims have come against Christians and are taking away their land or forcing them to pay a lot of money to keep the land they already own. These same people have threatened our pastor saying, "Unless you leave now—leave this village and the church—we will kidnap your wife and your daughter." As result, the pastor has had to leave for the security of his family. Now there is no pastor at the church and very few people attend it. A few come to pray and the church still needs to be finished.

Please pray for the church. As believers, we should pray. This is what we should do.

Fathi

THIS IS WHAT IS HAPPENING IN EGYPT AT THE MOMENT AND IT CAN HAPPEN TO ANYONE—ANYTIME, ANYWHERE.

ANYTIME, ANYWHERE

At the moment, we are experiencing a very difficult problem with the Muslim Brotherhood from a village in the region of Minya.

They call themselves "El-Ekwhan," (the Brotherhood) but actually they are very wicked. They came and claimed a piece of land owned by a Christian man. He used to have a lot of land in that village. So they came and put their hands on the land—they claimed it as squatters—with the intention of taking it over or stealing it. With guns and machetes they came against that Christian man.

He went with some of his friends and spoke with people who are in authority over this village. Those people came and pushed away the Salafis and the wicked people. They pushed them away from that land. But they said, "We will not leave this property unless the Christian owner pays us so much money." They made an agreement to talk about it. The Christian owner has some kind Muslim friends that will go with him to support him when they discuss this situation.

The wicked people made up some false documents saying, "We have documents to prove that this land originally goes back to us." But they are false documents intended to put pressure on the Christian owner to pay them what they want.

We pray that somehow God will help this brother when they meet, but we need help for the days ahead, too. This is what is happening in Egypt at the moment and it can happen to anyone—anytime, anywhere.

Hebah

> NOW, THEIR LIVES ARE CHANGED AND THEY
> ARE FINDING JOY MORE THAN EVER BEFORE.

HINDERING THE CHILDREN

I am a sister serving in the Sunday school of our church. We usually pass by the homes where children live in our area and invite them to join us. The children like going to our Sunday school, and even the parents are happy, because they are able to see the changes in their children's lives.

One day, the children suddenly stopped coming with us. We began to search for the reason why this happened. We learned that the Coptic Orthodox priest had gone to the parents and told them, "Don't allow your children to go to the Sunday school. They are bad people and if your children go there, they will go to hell. We will also prevent the prayers on your bodies when you die and you will enter hell, too." The parents apologized to us but refused to send their children.

We also noticed (among the very needy people) that the girls would come but would not pay attention to the Word of God in the church. When we asked them, they answered, "The priests told us not to hear your words but to just take the gifts from you." We explained to them that we are using the same Bible and some of them accepted Jesus in their life. Now, their lives are changed and they are finding joy more than ever before.

Nasser

> FOR THE SAKE OF CHRIST, THEN, I AM
> CONTENT WITH WEAKNESSES, INSULTS,
> HARDSHIPS, PERSECUTIONS, AND CALAMITIES.
> FOR WHEN I AM WEAK, THEN I AM STRONG.
> (2 CORINTHIANS 12:10 ESV)

A CONSTANT THREAT

My Christian friend in Upper Egypt, who is about 50 years old, was kidnapped. At the end of the day, he closed his shop and went home. While he was opening the gate of his home, three people, with their faces and heads covered, came and attacked him. They put him in a car at gunpoint, covered his head, and kidnapped him.

My friend had a large amount of money at that time. They called his family and asked for a ransom. His family collected all the money they asked for and agreed to meet in a certain place to give them the money. The kidnappers took the money and released him a short time later.

This is not the only story like this that I know. It happens almost daily, especially in Upper Egypt, and especially against Christians.

Fady

BUT IT ISN'T MAGICAL—IT IS SOMETHING SPIRITUAL. IT IS THE LORD AND THE TRUTH OF THE WORD OF GOD.

IT ISN'T MAGICAL

I am a physician, and one day during my hospital rounds, I was checking on a patient who had cirrhosis of the liver. He asked me if the disease would last forever. I told him that his disease, unfortunately, was chronic. He also had a hernia and asked if it was possible to have an operation to repair it. I told him it would be very difficult because the anesthesia could be even more harmful for his damaged liver.

The patient became very sad and I told him, "You know, Jesus is still alive and He can give you a new liver." I only meant to encourage him.

The patient then started to ask a question. "I know that Mousa (Moses), Isa (Jesus), and Mohammed all prophesied—"

And I told him, "No, it's not like Mousa and Mohammed. Jesus is special and His death is different. His life is different. All of the others had sins and problems during their lives. But Jesus is the only one who lived without any sin."

This was not planned on my part. I just started to talk with him.

Later, my director learned that I talked about Jesus with the patient and had me transferred from that hospital to a different one. He told me that the nurses wanted to kill me because I tried to encourage the patient. I was astonished at that. I was working in a teaching hospital and they transferred me to a rehabilitation hospital—a place where you teach people how to eat food and things like that. It was totally different. I'm a clinician.

I was afraid, of course, at that time. But God opened my eyes and heart to Psalm 105 where it says the Lord will never let other people oppress me.

I was disappointed to be away from my hospital, but six months later I was transferred back. When I came back, the staff looked at me through different eyes and they began to persecute me in every possible manner.

I had been back only a short time when it was discovered that the director of my hospital was a thief. Actually, it was not only him, but all of the people who had been involved in my transfer to the other hospital. Even those who just wrote a letter in support of my transfer—all were transferred to different hospitals. That's when my colleagues started to be afraid of me. They felt that no one could hurt me because there was something magical that protected me. But it isn't magical—it is something spiritual. It is the Lord and the truth of the Word of God.

I am still practicing at the hospital. The persecutions have started again, but they have not forgotten about me or the director and all of the others who were transferred and never returned.

Mamdouh

FORTY PERCENT OF WHAT WE GAINED
IN FREEDOM OVER THE YEARS HAS NOW
BEEN LOST. BUT ONE BENEFIT FROM THE
REVOLUTION IS THAT THE CHURCH
HAS STARTED PRAYING SERIOUSLY.

THE END OF THE WORLD

I am the chairman of a group of churches in Upper Egypt. One day, a family came to me saying, "Our daughter has been kidnapped." She is still gone. It has been more than a month. She is about 16 years old. We have no idea where she is or who has taken her. Then again, three days ago, a 13-year-old boy was kidnapped and we still have no idea about him. His best friend is one of my relatives.

There are many kidnappings in Egypt—not only of girls, but also of men. They are being kidnapped for money. If people pay the money, then sometimes the people come back. They usually have to pay somewhere between 20,000 and 30,000 Egyptian Pounds ($3,000—$4,500

USD). We don't really know who is doing the kidnappings, but we know that some members of the Muslim Brotherhood are doing it for money. And because poverty is growing day by day, this is one way of getting money out of Christians.

Recently, a prayer request was raised in our meeting. A property of more than 900 square meters (10,000 square feet) was taken away for the same purpose—for ransom. If they don't get money, they will turn it into a mosque. It has become very common now. We used to hear these things, and we would say, "I don't believe it." But now, almost every week we hear another story like this. It is very bad in all of the country right now—not just in Upper Egypt or Lower Egypt.

Many worshipers keep coming to our churches and are under tremendous stress. They come with many hurts inside. Many people come to pray, but they pray with a very troubled soul. Some Muslims also come and stand outside of our churches while we are singing and worshiping. But I don't know if they come as spies or if they are enjoying our worship. I really can't decide.

The revolution has taken us back at least 40 years. Or I could also say that 40 percent of what we gained in freedom over the years has now been lost. But one benefit from the revolution is that the church has started praying seriously. I believe the church is going through a moment that will not last for long. The circumstances we are going through at the moment are temporary. But unfortunately, I don't think the circumstances will be much better in the near future.

Actually, we believe the end will come very soon. One day it will be finished. We expect the Second Coming of Jesus Christ. I think this is the end of the world.

PART 2

THE MUSLIM BROTHERHOOD AND THE REVOLUTION

> THEY HATE HIM WHO REPROVES IN THE GATE, AND THEY ABHOR HIM WHO SPEAKS THE TRUTH.
> —AMOS 5:10 ESV

UNDERSTANDING WHAT HAS HAPPENED IN EGYPT

Many confusing reports about Egypt have been offered to the American people by both the media and our administration. Even those who are traditionally balanced, like the BBC, depict the Muslim Brotherhood to be peaceful demonstrators who are the victims of injustice.

These misperceptions have caused some to believe that recent events in Egypt were a "military coup" to depose a democratically elected president. After all, when a military intervenes in what appears to be a political situation, it does not seem to be a good thing. But knowing the background allows us to better understand and appreciate the events.

Please consider the following points to help clarify some of the situations Egypt has experienced since the Revolution of January 25, 2011:

- The Muslim Brotherhood refused to participate in the January 25, 2011, Revolution and called upon their followers to boycott it. Traditionally, they had made backroom deals with President Hosni Mubarak's administration and strongly felt that the revolution would not see the light of day. It was only when the revolution showed signs of success that they not only chose to participate, but claimed that they led it.[3]

- Mr. Morsi was in prison at the time of the 2011 Revolution. In cooperation with the Palestinian Hamas, a terrorist organization, Mr. Morsi and Hamas leaders allegedly attacked and killed many of the prison guards and escaped. Regardless of the cause of his imprisonment, there was no investigation regarding his escape and the murder of the guards as well as his plotting with a foreign government. He was only charged after his removal from office and is currently awaiting trial for those crimes.

- The Muslim Brotherhood did many illegal activities in order to win the election:

  > Allegedly accepted foreign aid from Qatar and other nations[4] to give food, money, and jobs to the poor and needy to buy their votes.[5]

  > Legally, religious political parties are banned in Egypt. That alone disqualified Mr. Morsi from running for election. But people feared the wrath of the Muslim Brotherhood so they did not oppose his nomination.

  > Election ballots were pre-printed with a check mark for Mr. Morsi.

> Prevented, by force, entire Christian villages from voting so that Mr. Morsi would win.[6]

> Closed down many election precincts early in areas that were not favorable to Mr. Morsi.

> The Muslim Brotherhood intimidated the police, military, and election board saying that Egypt would suffer a blood bath if Mr. Morsi did not win.[7]

> The Muslim Brotherhood declared Mr. Morsi a winner almost 24 hours before the actual declaration by the election committee.

- With the slimmest margin, 51.7% of 26.4 million votes,[8] Mohamed Morsi was declared the winner. Mr. Morsi and the Muslim Brotherhood took this as a mandate to do as they pleased with a "winner takes all" approach. He began to fire officials without cause, even those in judicial positions that he had no power over, and replaced them with his Muslim Brotherhood friends—regardless of their criminal records or violent histories.

- In November 2012, Mr. Morsi issued a decree to protect himself and his decisions from any review or challenge. He gave himself sweeping power to act without censure or balance of power, making himself like an infallible, modern-day Pharaoh.

- Mr. Morsi and his party (without a legislative branch) rushed into re-writing a pro-Islamic constitution that would ensure their indefinite stay in power despite the protests of minorities and boycotts by liberals, moderates, women, and Christian groups. It is worth noting that Mr. Morsi's new constitution made no provision of impeachment or for early election procedures.

- Mr. Morsi prevented the military from protecting Egyptian borders alongside Palestine (Hamas) and the Sudan (Halayeb Triangle), thereby giving up Egyptian land. Mr. Morsi allowed Al-Qaeda to set-up shop in the Sinai because he cared more about Pan Islam (the Islamic Union) than for the interests of Egypt. He restrained the Egyptian police and military from removing the criminal fanatic elements from the Sinai.

- While Mr. Morsi was in office the Egyptian economy suffered a serious decline; unemployment rose (more than 39% for males ages 20-24 and 60.5% for female youth in the same age bracket[9]), inflation skyrocketed, and there was a shortage of oil, electricity, and food. The economic and social affairs of the country were poorly managed because the only qualification of those he appointed was that they were members of the Muslim Brotherhood.

- In March 2013, the Egyptian people asked Morsi to change the direction of the country. For three months, Morsi refused. They gathered 22 million signatures (Morsi was elected with less than 13 million votes—more than half of those who voted for him signed the petition), asking Mr. Morsi to call for an early election or for him to resign. Once again, Mr. Morsi refused to call for a referendum on his presidency. This was confirmation that the Muslim Brotherhood was using the democracy to establish their own theocracy in Egypt.

- It is estimated by many Egyptians that more than 34 million citizens went to the streets on June 30, 2013, to demand the removal of Mr. Morsi. The Atlantic Wire reported an Egyptian military estimate of 14 million demonstrators.[10] At any rate, this was perhaps the largest gathering of people in the history of our planet. The Muslim Brotherhood and Mr. Morsi refused to respond to the will of the people and made it clear that they would either be in power or they would shed blood. The Muslim Brotherhood was capable of massacring great numbers of Egyptians. They had terrorists' shops in the Sinai and a stockpile of weapons acquired from Libya and Hamas.

- The Egyptian people begged the military to intervene and protect them from Mr. Morsi and the Muslim Brotherhood. For that reason, the military responded to the cry of the people. General Abdel-Fattah el-Sisi gave the administration numerous opportunities to fix the problems. When Mr. Morsi refused to respond, General el-Sisi gathered the moral, moderate, and religious leaders (including the Coptic Pope and the Islamic of the Grand Sheik of Al-Azhar), temporarily suspended the constitution, and appointed the head of the Supreme Court as the acting president until a democratic election could be held.[11]

- On July 3, 2013, the Egyptian people received General el-Sisi's "Declaration of Independence" from the Muslim Brotherhood with even more millions than those that had gathered on the June 30, 2013. It was a joyful night of festivity and fireworks.

- Since Mr. Morsi's ouster, the Muslim Brotherhood has been kidnapping[12] and torturing many innocent people; burning down churches and killing Christians in an attempt to intimidate the Egyptian people and return Mr. Morsi to power. However, the Muslim Brotherhood media machine paints another picture as though the military is attacking the Muslim Brotherhood. In reality, the Muslim Brotherhood has staged events where they killed their own people in order to convince the Western media that they were the victims. They are on a campaign to portray the Muslim Brotherhood as being massacred by the Egyptian authorities. Sadly, the Western media buys the stories as factual.

- In the days following Mr. Morsi's ouster, it is estimated that 113 churches were attacked. Many were burned to the ground. Thousands of Christian-owned businesses were destroyed and some Christians were gunned down at the doors of their churches. Unfortunately, our American media and government have closed their ears and eyes to the cries of the terrified 15 million Christians in Egypt and appear eager to protect the Muslim Brotherhood.

The Muslim Brotherhood has made it clear that they will get their revenge. They attack anything and anyone who does not support their cause. The shedding of blood seems to be the only thing that quenches their thirst for power and most Egyptian people live in fear of them. Many have been afraid to go to their jobs, churches, or even to the market to shop.

Please pray that the Lord would give Christians peace in their hearts and for the protection of His people in Egypt from the wrath of the defeated Satan!

THE EFFECT OF
FLAWED POLICIES

THE FREEDOM AND JUSTICE PARTY

The Muslim Brotherhood was outlawed up until the time that President Hosni Mubarak was ousted in January 2011. They were not actually legitimized following the revolution. They were still illegal, but it came to the point where no one chose (out of fear) to prosecute their followers.

While they were still outlawed, they found a way to get around the law in the event that anyone would oppose them. They created a party called the Freedom and Justice Party that became their political arm. Many people were concerned about this and would say, "It's against the law. You can't function as a party." But they would say, "No, no, no. We're not functioning. There is a party doing the work. It's called Hizb Al-Horria Wal-'Adala." The reality is that they are the political cover for the Muslim Brotherhood.

El-Ekhwan is an Arabic term. The root of it means "The Brotherhood." Nowadays, its exclusive meaning is the Muslim Brotherhood. Some of the Christians call them "the wicked ones," "the bad ones," or "the haters" and use the same term without distinguishing one from the other. In their minds, they are all evil.

Perhaps they see them that way because of the intimidation tactics the Muslim Brotherhood is using so effectively. It is like guerilla warfare. Sometimes, when they kidnap a person and kill them, they will cut off all of their fingers at the knuckles and cut off their nose. It makes one wonder if they are really human beings? It is so awful and so hard to believe they could do those things to another man. Unfortunately, the West has not been seeing those kinds of pictures. The Egyptian government is now on a campaign to show the pictures and the videos to the world.

AMERICA'S SUPPORT OF THE MUSLIM BROTHERHOOD

In recent months we've been asked many times, "Why does the U.S. want to support the Muslim Brotherhood?" It is a very good question with at least a couple of explanations.

Before the U.S. invaded Iraq, President George W. Bush operated from this premise: If the Arab people had the opportunity, they would elect a democratic system of governance. If they could choose, they would choose a system of democracy. But, after our experience in Iraq and many other places, we discovered that in Arab nations, predominantly populated by Muslims, they would in most cases choose to elect an Islamic system of government.

In our opinion this happens for any of three reasons:

1. The Muslim Brotherhood convinces the poor that their economic condition can only be blamed on the fact that the country is not following the pure Islamic law. "If we follow the pure ways of Islam, we would have the wealth of oil-rich Arab nations."

2. Founded in 1928, the Muslim Brotherhood has a well-organized structure that enables them to be more effective campaigners and more easily reach the masses.

3. The Muslim Brotherhood has far more resources available to them than any one party in any given Islamic-majority country; especially after a revolution or a war that would destroy the existing majority party.

Then, there came a change in U.S. administrations and a major shift in thinking and policies. President Obama realized that if you give Muslims a chance to vote, they are going to choose an Islamic form of government. In an attempt to be preemptive, Mr. Obama decided to position himself in support of the Islamists; regardless of their values or what they stood for. He knew they would be the ones to assume power and he would be on their good side. From the very beginning, he wanted to be perceived as a supporter of the Muslim Brotherhood and their causes.

This is why support has gone out to the Muslim Brotherhood and to the fanatics in Egypt, Tunisia, and Syria. What's happening now in Syria is that the Muslim Brotherhood is waiting in the wings to assume power as soon as they overthrow President Bashar Assad.

This is why, from the very beginning, the response from this administration has been very ambiguous at best. They looked at Egypt and did not want to give up their "golden cow" (the Muslim Brotherhood). They doubled-down on the Muslim Brotherhood with the idea that all of the Arab nations would follow the Egyptian model. They have been taken off-guard because they did not expect the counter-revolution to happen. The plan was that everything would go to the Islamists, who in turn would help accomplish Mr. Obama's agenda for the Middle East and Arab nations.

No one would have expected or imagined the Egyptian people could be successful in removing the Muslim Brotherhood from power. The Muslim Brotherhood made it clear: "We waited for more than 80 years to rule Egypt, and we will not give up power for the next 500 years." After the removal of President Morsi, a prominent Egyptian Christian leader commented on the event: "This is the miracle of all miracles!" To most observers, removing President Morsi and the Muslim Brotherhood from power was an implausible event.

Many of the Egyptian people were very unhappy that the U.S. seemed to be in the pockets of the Islamists. It appears that the Obama administration, over and over again, supported the Muslim Brotherhood regardless of what they did. The Muslim Brotherhood would kill Christians, but no one would hear an official condemnation and outcry. The Muslim Brotherhood would kill the young people who were saying, "You can't do this. We want freedom." The West, neither in words or any meaningful action, answered the cries of the majority of the Egyptian people.

There is another possible explanation for why the U.S. was so favorable toward the Muslim Brotherhood. There are allegations that a secret document was drawn between Presidents Obama and Morsi, where Mohamed Morsi gave up 20 percent of the Sinai desert area to the Palestinians allowing them to move and live in it. This was meant to solve the problem with Israel.[13] Consequently, President Obama had the idea that the Muslim Brotherhood had influence over Muslims all over the world. There are many such conspiracy theories being alleged in Egypt; many of which cannot be substantiated.

It was just a few weeks after Mr. Morsi was declared the President of Egypt that the Israelis were being shelled by the Palestinians. As soon as President Morsi intervened, the Palestinians stopped shelling Israel until the day of he was removed from power.

At that time, President Obama was campaigning for his reelection. Obama's ability to use President Morsi to influence Hammas to stop the shelling repositioned President Obama as an influential world leader and a hero. He saw a boost in his numbers and gained much credibility in the process because he was supposedly able to stop Hamas and the Palestinians from attacking Israel. President Obama then decided to use the Muslim Brotherhood to execute his agenda for all of the Middle East. It's important for people to realize that there are elements of the Muslim Brotherhood in every country—in every Islamic state in the Middle East.

It is apparent that President Obama's mentality has been that he would control the Middle East through the Muslim Brotherhood. It is rumored that the U.S. Administration sent large sums of money to help Mr. Morsi's election campaign. That money was then used to influence the votes of the majority under-privileged population by giving-out groceries and cash assistance.

QATAR PLAYS BOTH SIDES

Qatar is a very small state with a great deal of ambition with roots in the Muslim Brotherhood. For some reason,

Qatar has played a significant role. Through their media machine, Al-Jazeera channels large financial gifts to the Egyptian Muslim Brotherhood.

A few months ago, a prominent religious leader (and a very reliable source) met with an assistant to the American Ambassador to Egypt and posed this question: "Does the U.S. support the Muslim Brotherhood with financial resources?"

The answer was, "No. However, we encourage the Qataris to support them."

How does the U.S. encourage the Qataris to do that? America has a base in Qatar. It seems as if they would do anything for the U.S. and there is strong allegation of money being transferred from the U.S. to Qatar to pass on to the Muslim Brotherhood in Egypt. That money supposedly went for the support of the election of Mohamed Morsi.

That is how most of the Egyptian people came to see President Morsi in the lap of the Obama administration—more so than in any other previous Egyptian administration.

THE UNDESIRABLE AMBASSADOR

During this time, the U.S. Ambassador in Egypt, Ann Patterson, also became involved. She had her hands in almost everything and has caused the people of Egypt to hate President Obama and to hate the Ambassador even more than they hate the Muslim Brotherhood. The most hated people in Egypt today are not the Muslim Brotherhood, even though they have committed many crimes. It is President Barack Obama and the American administration, including Ambassador Patterson. Her presence in Egypt has been declared "undesirable." In the history of Egyptian-American relations there has never been an ambassador so unpopular or who was requested to be removed from their diplomatic post.

Ann Patterson was a career diplomat who entered foreign service in 1973. She served in various capacities and many roles. One of her recent and more significant roles was her appointment in 2007 as the U.S. Ambassador to Pakistan. Her experience in volatile countries like Colombia and Pakistan made her an ideal diplomat on paper during a time of volatile transition. On June 30, 2011, congress confirmed her nomination by Mr. Obama to become the U.S. Ambassador to Egypt—exactly one year to the date before Mr. Morsi assumed office. Ms. Patterson was regarded by Egyptians as the person responsible for America's close embrace of Islamists in Egypt.

While serving as the U.S. Ambassador, Ann Patterson would not meet with many government officials, but would meet with the leaders of the religious arm of the

Muslim Brotherhood. She would not meet with the president, but she would meet with the leaders who had influence upon him. Ms. Patterson unconditionally supported Mr. Morsi and the Muslim Brotherhood's actions and never criticized any of their policies or violence against the demonstrators!

Egyptians could have tolerated anything but the public discouragement of the June 30 protest and the removal of Mr. Morsi. In a speech given by Patterson on June 18, 2013, she attempted to put a damper on the revolution by saying, "Some say that street action will produce better results than elections. To be honest, my government and I are deeply skeptical."[14]

After the removal of Mr. Morsi, El Fagr News reported that Ms. Patterson, in a telephone conversation with General Abdul Fatah el-Sisi, demanded that he release all Muslim Brotherhood members held for questioning: "And when Sisi rejected this order, the American ambassador began threatening him that Egypt will turn into another Syria and live through a civil war, to which Sisi responded violently: 'Neither you nor your country can overcome Egypt and its people.'" The same news article reported that General Sisi, when responding to Patterson's demands to release the Muslim Brotherhood from jail and the dismissal of all charges, said to her, "Stop meddling in our affairs. The Egyptian people are capable of looking after their own welfare."[15]

Her declared support of the Muslim Brotherhood and relentless attempts to keep them in power against the will of the Egyptian people made her the most disliked foreign political figure in Egypt. By and large, Egyptians rejected her and demanded her departure. On August 1, 2013, Ms. Patterson was nominated to serve as the Assistant Secretary of State in the State Department's Bureau of Near Eastern Affairs which oversees the Middle East.

Mrs. Clinton Misses an Opportunity

This account also comes from the very reliable source mentioned earlier. On July 16, 2012, while Hillary Clinton was the Secretary of State, she made a visit to Egypt at the request of Ambassador Patterson. It was the worst visit of Mrs. Clinton's term of service. The people of Alexandria greeted her by throwing tomatoes at her limousine. The people were chanting, "Monica! Monica! Monica!"—taunting her about Monica Lewinsky. And what was Hillary Clinton's answer to their chants? She said, "I felt so bad that good tomatoes were wasted."[16]

During her visit, she had a meeting with the Christian leadership of Egypt. The only ones present were Mrs. Clinton, the ambassador, and the Egyptian Christian leaders—no one else. Those leaders grilled her with questions to the point that she appeared to be very uncomfortable. One of the Christian leaders in that meeting asked, "How can you support the Muslim Brotherhood? Did you support Morsi to come to power? Did you not know the mistakes that you were making?"

Mrs. Clinton's answer was, "I understand we have made some mistakes." Then they asked the follow-up question, "How are you going to fix it?" Her answer was, "Well, by the end of the year, if President Obama is re-elected, I will not renew in my position. The person who will come after me is going to have to fix it."

Another of the Christian leaders asked: "You invaded Iraq. Most of the Christians were persecuted and were pushed out of the country. You helped the revolution in Libya. Most of the Christians were kicked out. You are helping the fighters in Syria. Most of the Christians are becoming refugees and Syria has very little or no Christians now. What are your plans for the Egyptian Christians?" She answered, "I will not stay in my post after the election. We have definitely made some mistakes."

Another question focused on how she could have one of her advisors, her deputy chief of staff, with long-standing ties to the Muslim Brotherhood? They told Secretary Clinton, "Of course, she will only feed you the information that the Muslim Brotherhood wants for you to know." Her comment was that the woman was an honorable woman and that she would like for the leaders to meet her. At the end of the meeting she called the woman in. That woman, Huma Abedin, is married to

Anthony Weiner, the man who resigned from Congress after a "sexting scandal" and who recently ran unsuccessfully for the office of mayor of New York City. The Egyptian Christian leaders were shocked and humiliated when Secretary Clinton, to their face, brought in Huma Abedin in order to introduce her to them.

A Damaged Relationship

The relationship between Egypt and the U.S. is very, very damaged and the Russians couldn't be more pleased. When the U.S. says, "We're going to call this a coup and we're not going to give you any more aid," the Russians then say to the Egyptians, "You don't need the U.S. We're going to stand with you." That's why the Obama administration has been trying to walk such a fine line. They've been saying, "It is a coup. No, it isn't a coup. We're going to cut the aid. No, we're not going to cut the aid."

In this post-cold war era, the American administration is afraid that, if they pull their hands out of Egypt, the Russians will have a great alliance with the Egyptian people. The Chinese are doing the same. They have not been too quick to say it is a coup, either. So, the American administration feels like they are backed into a corner. Basically, the position they had with the Muslim Brotherhood now requires them to take the totally opposite position.

In modern Egyptian history, there has never been a time that the sentiment toward the U.S. has been as negative as it is today.

Just a little more than four years ago, at Cairo University (June 4, 2009), there was a great hope in the person of Barack Hussein Obama. The Egyptian people finally felt that the person who was going to fix all of the problems; the person who was going to take care of the Muslims; the person who was going to be fair in the Middle East; the person who had an Islamic history had arrived. They thought he would be their savior. There was never a U.S. president who was adored by the Egyptians as much as President Obama was adored. There was never as much hope in anybody than the hope they had in President Obama.

But the strong feeling from that time has been replaced by an even stronger feeling now. There is disappointment in the things he said he would do but did not do and anger at his silence. Neither the moderates nor the Christians in Egypt can understand him and ask, "How can you support an organization that is the mother of Al-Qaeda—the ones who encourage attacking the West? How can you stand with them against the moderates and the Christians?"

There is a saying in the Middle East that goes like this: "My brother and I against my cousin; my cousin and I against a stranger." It seems as if the U.S. didn't understand that. The Muslim Brotherhood was going to partner with them for their own benefit. But, once the benefit was gone they were going to turn on them. That's the lesson we should have learned from the Afghanis. They will have a partnership with you now for their own benefit. However, once they don't need you and there is no benefit from you, they're going to turn on you. President Obama did not recognize that.

The Saudis came out a few days after the removal of Morsi and made it clear that they would stand with the military in Egypt against the Muslim Brotherhood and the violence. The people from Jordan and Bahrain quickly supported the position of the Saudis. The Saudis even had a meeting with the French Foreign Minister and explained Egypt's position, telling them, "If you do any kind of a punishment against Egypt, you can count this as a punishment on the Saudis." They are on a campaign to explain to the West the dirty ways of the Muslim Brotherhood.

We anticipate that healing with the U.S. is going to take some time. We anticipate that the government in Egypt will want to be open-handed and democratic, but we believe they will have to use a strong hand to be able to control the elements of the Muslim Brotherhood.

Violence Against Moderates and Christians

The violence by the Muslim Brotherhood is not only a harmful act in itself, but it is done in a way to scare and intimidate the Egyptian people. Massacring people is just one example.

After the dismissal of the demonstrators on August 14, 2013, members of the Muslim Brotherhood went to a police station in an area called Kerdesa in the state of Giza, just outside of Cairo, and took eleven policemen and severely tortured them. To scare off the moderate Egyptians, the Muslim Brotherhood used inhuman methods of torture. Many bodies were disfigured after being slaughtered and the lucky ones who were able to escape were missing body parts. The Muslim Brotherhood wanted to make an example so that the rest of the people would be intimated and would not oppose them.

On August 19, 2013, 25 soldiers were killed in the Sinai Peninsula in an ambush by the Muslim Brotherhood. They were all about 21 years old and were getting their final release after completing their mandatory service in the military. The militant Muslim Brotherhood made the 25 young men lie on the ground and then shot them all in the back of the head through their skulls. The 26th person was made to witness the atrocity committed against his co-workers. He was sent to tell the story of what could be expected from the Muslim Brotherhood: they would terrorize the Egyptian people, especially those serving in the military.

On August 6, 2013, a 10 year-old girl named Jessica (Jessie) was on her way home with a friend of her mother's after finishing the 9th day of a 10-day vacation Bible School. Suddenly, one single shot to the heart ended her life. The little girl was no threat to the Muslim Brotherhood. Her murder serves as a reminder that they will kill indiscriminately, torture, and massacre whomever and whenever they wish.

The cry from the media in Egypt (even from the spokesperson for the president) is: "In the past, when there was harm to one of the churches we heard the West go crazy. We heard the American administration and human rights organizations condemn us. But now, with the burning of more than 110 churches and attacks on so many of the homes and businesses of Christians, where is the West? Where is the U.S.? Where is the outcry that this is not good? Where is President Obama?"

In the previous administration it was clear that you couldn't abuse the minorities. But now, even on CNN, the report is mentioned merely as a statement. Then they go on to point out with great coverage how the moderate government is unfairly arresting and torturing the innocent and peaceful Muslim Brotherhood. The truth of the matter is that the Muslim Brotherhood has committed many atrocities and then blamed it on the government.

WHAT HAPPENS NEXT?

Were an election to be held today, we do not believe the Muslim Brotherhood would regain power—especially not the presidency. Maybe they would have some seats in the parliament. There are some pockets and villages in the south were the Muslim Brotherhood has brainwashed the poor and uneducated.

The problem is, even in the presidential election and the voting on the constitution, the cities with the most educated people did not vote for the Muslim Brotherhood. But, the places where farmers and poor people live—where votes can be bought with cash, meat, rice and groceries—voted for Morsi. The places where they could stop the Christians from voting—those places voted for the Muslim Brotherhood. So, although some of the people in the villages will vote for them, they will never be in the majority. Furthermore, the activities the Muslim Brotherhood are doing now—killing of the soldiers, kidnapping and killing Christians, burning their homes and businesses, and attacks on the churches—are causing the moderates and those who are in between to say, "We are not going to vote for you anymore. We will get you out of power, even if it means you are going to kill us and kill our kids, it won't change our minds. We are not going to put you in power again."

THE GOSPEL IS BEING ADVANCED

One would think with the suffering of the believers in Egypt, Christianity would be weakened. Since the election of Mr. Morsi and the Muslim Brotherhood, violent elements have launched major attacks on Egyptian Christians, their businesses, homes, and churches. These attacks have intensified since the June 2013 Revolution. There are countless documented destructions of homes and businesses owned by Christians. Human lives and the source of livelihood for thousands of Christians have been shattered without any reparation. Many Christians have been kidnapped, tormented, and released only after paying the demanded large ransoms. Some Christians have suffered to the point of death simply for the sake of the Gospel.

Juicy Ecumenism (The Institute on Religion & Democracy's Blog) reported, "St. George Coptic Catholic Church was set upon by over 500 jihadists on July 3, just after the successful 'People's Coup' against Morsi. The priest in charge, Father Ayoub Youssef, reported that the church was 'systematically' looted — down to the toys and electrical wiring from the walls. 'After they made sure they looted everything, they poured gasoline on foam mattresses and 3,000 books in the library, and set the place on fire,' he recounted. Amazingly, after the August 14 crackdown on the Islamists' demonstrations, 'they were much harsher,' he said. At that point calls were sent via mosque loudspeakers 'urging Muslims to wage jihad in support of Muslims.' They attacked and destroyed the Virgin Mary and St. Abram Monastery in Delga, and beheaded a Coptic barber, Iskander Tous, and mutilated his body."[17]

Some towns and villages were turned into a form of concentration camps, terrifying and tormenting their Christian residents. More than 110 churches were burned down to the ground or severely damaged. Some churches were ransacked and looted while the contents of other churches were brought out and set on fire. Bibles, song books, benches, chairs, and fans were defiled and burned.

One would expect the condition of a church in such an environment to be weak and ineffective. Not so! Just like Paul wrote, "I want you to know, brothers, that what has happened to me has really served to advance the gospel" (Philippians 1:12 NIV). Paul had been imprisoned by the Roman authorities for preaching the gospel. Although it would seem that imprisoning such a leader would impede the advancement of the gospel, Paul reported that it had the opposite effect. Like Jesus, Paul didn't consider his suffering his own but recognized it as a part of God's greater purpose to reveal his glory—the greatest blessing he could bestow on his people. This oriented Paul's eyes toward the opportunities God would lay at his feet in each difficult circumstance so that the mission of Christ's gospel would be advanced.

Egyptian Christians have exhibited great maturity in the Lord and they have seen their suffering as a means to reflect God's love and advance the Gospel. This has caused many Muslims to be open to the Good News.

In an interview with the Pope of the Coptic Orthodox Church (approximately 90 percent of Egyptian Christians are Coptic Orthodox—about 13 million people), reporters set a trap by asking him, "With all of the violence against Christians and churches in Egypt why haven't you called on Western protection?"

Pope Tawadros responded, "We are all Egyptians and do not need an outside intervention. If they burn all church buildings—buildings can be replaced—a single soul, Christian or Muslim, is far more important than all buildings." Such a positive response had endeared the Pope to the larger Muslim population and has opened them for the Gospel.

In a recent interview with CBN News, Jessica's parents (the 10-year-old child gunned down by the militant members of the Muslim Brotherhood) said, "After the loss of our daughter by the Muslim Brotherhood, we have decided to pray for Muslims, and even to pray for those who have murdered our daughter." The reporter then asked the parents, "Do you forgive your daughter's killers?" They answered, "Because of Christ, we do forgive them."[18]

God is doing many things that we can't write for the protection of people on the ground. But, we can tell you that this is an exciting time to be alive and a part of what God is doing in the Middle East, North Africa, and the Arab world. Would you join us in praying for that part of the world?

POSTSCRIPT: THE SYRIA CONNECTION

Everyone knows it; the Middle East is complicated. But the Arab Spring has made it even more complex. At one time the policies and role of the U.S. was clear when dealing with those we supported and those considered our enemies. However, the lack of decisive action by our current administration and befriending our traditional enemies has been confusing to many in the Middle East. The support of President Obama's administration for the Muslim Brotherhood gives Russia an advantage that puts our country behind the "8-ball." The civil war that has raged since March 2011 in Syria clearly illustrates this point.

We unambiguously condemn the use of chemical or biological weapons, regardless of whether they are used by the Syrian government, the opposition, or any other party. It remains unclear who was responsible for the chemical weapons used in the Ghouda attack on August 21, 2013. The Syrian government accuses the opposition and the opposition is pointing a finger at the Syrian government. Incidentally, the opposition is led in large by the Muslim Brotherhood who is known to justify killing their own supporters to serve their greater purpose. They are media savvy and masters in setting traps or staging events for their own benefit.

Would the Muslim Brotherhood really have used chemical weapons on their own people? Yes, especially if killing a few hundred of their own people would have caused the U.S. to attack the Syrian armed forces and hasten the Muslim Brotherhood's overthrow of the government. The ultimate beneficiary of a U.S. strike on Syria would have been the Muslim Brotherhood who is waiting to take control of Syria.

It is ironic that President Obama condemned former President George W. Bush for acting alone on some issues. Then-Senator Obama lectured us on how he would have built a coalition leading up to the war in Iraq. But as president, he was willing to act without the support of most of the international community when dealing with Syria. President Obama's disappointing decisions has given Russia the opportunity to lead on Syrian issues and they now have a "win-win" situation.

Because of President Obama's weakened position in the Middle East, we were left with the following undesirable outcomes when addressing the use of chemical weapons in Syria:

• The Syrian government used chemical weapons. They could surrender them to the control of the international community and never use them again.

In this scenario, Russia would be shown as the leader. The U.S. would save face for not ordering the airstrike and the future of the Muslim Brotherhood potentially leading Syria would be unknown.

- The Syrian government did not use chemical weapons. To avoid an airstrike they could agree to the Russian proposal for control by the international community. This scenario would also position Russia as the diplomatic leader. The U.S. would save face for not ordering the airstrike and the future of the Muslim Brotherhood potentially leading Syria would remain unknown.

- The Syrian government refuses to accept responsibility, either because they are guilty or because it was the Muslim Brotherhood who used the chemical weapons. With this scenario, Russia would be shown as the leader for trying a high-profile attempt for peace. The U.S. would have carried out airstrikes and would have hastened the Muslim Brotherhood coming to power in Syria.

We do not like dictators in power, but our administration needs to understand that President Bashar al-Assad is a moderate bully in comparison to the tyrannical monster of the Muslim Brotherhood.

Many Americans do not know that it was the offspring of the Muslim Brotherhood who murdered the former

Egyptian President Anwar Sadat for making peace with Israel; or that Al-Qaeda is a daughter organization of the Muslim Brotherhood. In fact, Ayman Al-Zawahiri (the current leader of Al-Qaida) cut his teeth as an extremist when he was a member of the Muslim Brotherhood. His younger brother, Mohammed Al-Zawahiri—one of the unofficial leaders/fighters and supporters of ousted Egyptian President Morsi—was recently arrested for violent attacks on Egyptians.

Considering that virtually every attack on U.S. interests by extremists was somehow associated with the Muslim Brotherhood, our support of them has been mind-baffling for those who are conscious of its history. There must be options other than destroying the Syrian military and facilitating an even bigger tyrant (the Muslim Brotherhood) to replace them.

We need to pray for the hearts of our administration and the Syrian leaders to be softened and opened to the Lord. Pray for the deliverance of the Syrian people who have suffered the loss of more than 120,000 lives and been tormented for nearly three years. May the Lord hasten the end of their displacement and suffering and may they come to know Him in a deep and personal way!

END NOTES

[1] Many Christians in Egypt estimate their numbers at 18% of the population (15.4 million). Conservative Muslims report the Christian population at no higher than 8% (6.8 million).

[2] Legal Information Institute. Adverse Possession. http://www.law.cornell.edu/wex/adverse_possession.

[3] http://analysisintelligence.com/intelligence-analysis/rise-of-the-muslim-brotherhood-in-context-of-the-egyptian-revolution/

[4] In the online issue of Western Journalism of August 31, 2013 – Kris Zane asserts that, "Investigative journalist Jerome Corsi has obtained a copy of the document held by the Egyptian military, proving the Obama regime sent millions of dollars in bribes to the Muslim Brotherhood." http://www.westernjournalism.com/uncovered-muslim-brotherhood-documents-put-obama-prison

[5] http://www.raymondibrahim.com/from-the-arab-world/did-the-muslim-brotherhood-really-win-egypts-presidency/

[6] Zaimov, Stoyan. The Christian Post, July 9, 2013. http://digital.ahram.org.eg/Policy.aspx?Serial=938414

[7] http://www.raymondibrahim.com/from-the-arab-world/did-the-muslim-brotherhood-really-win-egypts-presidency/

[8] Of the 26,420,763 votes cast, Mohamed Morsi received 13,203,131 and Ahmed Shaflik received 12,347,380; An additional 843,252 votes were declared invalid. Aljazeera. Celebration in Egypt as Morsi declared Winner. June 24, 2012. http://www.aljazeera.com/news/middleeast/2012/06/2012624124 45190400.html.

[9] Barsoum, Ghada. Cairo Review of Global Affairs: The American University in Cairo. No Jobs and Bad Jobs, July 12, 2013. http://www.aucegypt.edu/gapp/cairoreview/pages/articleDetails.aspx?aid=280

[10] http://www.theatlanticwire.com/global/2013/06/heres-what-todays-massive-anti-morsi-protests-egypt-looked/66728

[11] http://bigstory.ap.org/article/statement-egypts-military-chief

[12] Countless kidnapping stories are documented, especially in the Mina area!

[13] http://www.westernjournalism.com/uncovered-muslim-brotherhood-documents-put-obama-prison

14 Al-Fagr. Egyptian Activists Express Outrage Over U.S. Ambassador's Criticism of Protests, June 22, 2013. http://new.elfagr.org/Detail.aspx?nwsId=366503&seci d=24&vid=2

15 Al-Fagr. American Ambassador Threatens Sisi and the Team, July 11, 2013. http://new.elfagr.org/Detail. aspx?nwsId=380353&secid=1&vid=2

16 Catherine Chomiak. NBCNews.com. Clinton Says Egypt's Tomato Tossing Protesters Didn't Bother Her, July 16, 2012. http://worldnews.nbcnews.com/_news/ 2012/07/16/12774469-clinton-says-egypts-tomato-tossing-protesters-didnt-bother-her

17 McDonnel, Faith. Juicy Ecumenism - The Institute on Religion and Democracy's Blog. Egyptian Army Plays Cavalry – Takes Back Town From Islamists, Sept 17, 2013. http://juicyecumenism.com/2013/09/17/egypt-ian-army-plays-cavalry-takes-town-back-from-islamists/

18 Thomas, George. The Christian Broadcasting Network. Killing Egypt's Christians: She Was Our Only Little Child, November 9, 2013. http://www.cbn. com/cbnnews/world/2013/November/Egypt-Copts-Still-Threatened-by-Islamic-Insurgency/